HELP the ENVIRONMENT with Crafts

by Ruthie Van Oosbree

a Capstone company — publishers for children

Raintree is an imprint of Capstone Global Library Limited, a company incorporated in England and Wales having its registered office at 264 Banbury Road, Oxford, OX2 7DY – Registered company number: 6695582

www.raintree.co.uk
myorders@raintree.co.uk

Text © Capstone Global Library Limited 2025
The moral rights of the proprietor have been asserted.

All rights reserved. No part of this publication may be reproduced in any form or by any means (including photocopying or storing it in any medium by electronic means and whether or not transiently or incidentally to some other use of this publication) without the written permission of the copyright owner, except in accordance with the provisions of the Copyright, Designs and Patents Act 1988 or under the terms of a licence issued by the Copyright Licensing Agency, 5th Floor, Shackleton House, 4 Battle Bridge Lane, London, SE1 2HX (www.cla.co.uk). Applications for the copyright owner's written permission should be addressed to the publisher.

Edited by Jessica Rusick
Designed by Sarah DeYoung and Denise Hamernik
Media Research by Rebekah Hubstenberger
Projects by Ruthie Van Oosbree and Chelsey Luciow
Originated by Capstone Global Library Ltd

ISBN 978 1 3982 5562 3

British Library Cataloguing in Publication Data
A full catalogue record for this book is available from the British Library.

Acknowledgements
We would like to thank the following for permission to reproduce photographs:
Adobe Stock: Studio Romantic, 4; Mighty Media, Inc.: project photos. Design elements: iStockphoto: Bakai, Dmytro Synelnychenko, mightyisland; Mighty Media, Inc.

Every effort has been made to contact copyright holders of material reproduced in this book. Any omissions will be rectified in subsequent printings if notice is given to the publisher.

All the internet addresses (URLs) given in this book were valid at the time of going to press. However, due to the dynamic nature of the internet, some addresses may have changed, or sites may have changed or ceased to exist since publication. While the author and publisher regret any inconvenience this may cause readers, no responsibility for any such changes can be accepted by either the author or the publisher.

Printed and bound in India.

Contents

Crafting for the environment. 4
Toadstool house 6
Recycled rug. 8
Funky feeders 10
Flutter-by window sticker 12
Seedlings to share 14
Seed bombs 16
Cool composting. 18
Earth cake pops 20
Vertical garden 24
Self-watering planter pals 28
   Find out more 32
   About the author 32

Crafting for the environment

Do you want to change the world? Start with the environment! Whether you're hoping to reduce waste, grow more greenery or help local wildlife, the crafts in this book will make a difference to Mother Earth. Plus, these projects are good fun to make and share. You'll love helping the environment with crafts!

What is craftivism?

Craftivism is the act of using crafts to make a change in your community. It is short for "craft activism". People make crafts to protest against issues, draw attention to causes and help build a better world. Craftivism can be used for social justice, environmentalism, peace, political change and more. Use the projects in this book to become a craftivist for the environment!

BASIC SUPPLIES

food colouring *
hammer and nail *
hot glue gun * felt-tip pens *
paint and paintbrush *
pen and pencil *
recyclables * ruler *
glue * scissors

Craftivism tips

1. Prepare. Collect all your materials and supplies and read through the instructions carefully before starting a project. Cover your workspace with newspaper or another covering to protect it from spills.

2. Ask first. Before you start crafting, get permission to use any supplies you find.

3. Stay safe. Ask an adult for help using hot or sharp tools or hammers. Place scrap wood under items before hammering holes into them to protect surfaces.

4. Clean up. Tidy up after you've finished crafting. Put supplies back where you found them and clean up your workspace.

5. Keep it temporary. Craftivism projects shouldn't permanently alter public spaces. Respect these spaces and be considerate of other people!

Toadstool house

Offer frogs and toads a charming, mushroom-inspired cottage where they can take shelter from the hot Sun and predators.

Supplies

- hair dryer
- plastic planter about 15 centimetres in diameter
- craft knife
- ruler
- paint (white, brown, yellow, red, black) and paintbrushes
- large plastic bowl
- hot glue gun
- pebbles
- plastic cup
- leaves
- large, shallow dish
- water

1. Set the hair dryer to a high heat. Blow the hot air on one side of the planter for 15 to 30 seconds to soften the plastic.

2. Use the craft knife to carefully carve an arch about 7.5 to 10 cm across out of the warmed side.

3. Mix white paint with small amounts of brown and yellow to create a cream colour. Paint the planter cream. Paint the bowl red. Let both dry.

4. Paint white polka dots on the bowl and black or brown windows on the planter.

5. Use the hot glue gun to glue small pebbles around the arch to frame the doorway. Glue larger pebbles around the bottom of the planter.

6. Glue pebbles on top of the planter to help weigh it down. Make sure the pebbles don't overlap the edge. Glue the plastic cup upside down over the pebbles.

7. Glue the bowl rim-side down to the bottom of the plastic cup.

8. Place the house in a shady spot outside. Put leaves inside for bedding and leave a large, shallow dish filled with water near by.

Recycled rug

We throw away millions of tonnes of textiles, mostly clothing, every year. Rescue clothes that can't be donated from the landfill by transforming them into a cool textured rug!

Supplies
* old T-shirts in multiple colours
* scissors
* ruler
* piece of fabric about 50 cm by 50 cm
* chalk
* hot glue gun

1. Cut strips of fabric from a T-shirt. They should be about 2.5 to 5 cm wide.

2. Tie the strips together end to end to make a chain about 1 metre long.

3. Cut additional strips from 10 to 15 T-shirts. Cut the strips so they are 15 cm long.

4. Tie the T-shirt strips from step 3 onto the chain from step 2, varying the colours as you go.

5. Fold the piece of fabric into quarters. Use chalk to draw a quarter-circle on top. Cut the chalk line through all four layers. Unfold the fabric piece. It should now be a circle.

6. Use the hot glue gun to glue one end of the T-shirt chain to the centre of the circle. Wrap the chain in a spiral going outwards from the centre, gluing it down as you go. Leave about 5 cm of space around the edge of the circle.

7. Cut the edge of the circle into tassels by cutting inwards every 2.5 to 5 cm. Knot the tassels together two at a time. Your recycled rug is ready to display!

Funky feeders

Help birds get through the colder months with bird-seed decorations that hang on trees. As a bonus, you'll get to spot all kinds of feathered friends stopping by for a snack!

Supplies

- baking tray
- greaseproof paper
- non-stick cooking spray
- measuring jug and scales
- saucepan
- whisk
- mixing bowl
- silicone spatula
- 2 or more sticks
- cling film
- string
- scissors
- masking tape
- wooden beads

Ingredients

- 120 millilitres water
- 45 ml golden syrup
- 12 g unflavoured gelatine
- 175 g plain flour
- 380 g bird seed

1. Line the baking tray with greaseproof paper and spray with non-stick cooking spray.

2. Combine the water and golden syrup in the saucepan. Bring the mixture to a boil over high heat. Reduce the heat to low and whisk in the gelatine. Remove the pan from heat when the gelatine dissolves.

3. Pour the mixture into the mixing bowl. Add the flour and bird seed and mix with the silicone spatula.

4. Use cling film to mould scoops of the birdseed mix around the centre of each stick. Let the bird seed set on the baking tray overnight.

5. Tie two pieces of string onto the sides of one stick, leaving long ends above and below. Wrap a piece of masking tape around the bottom ends and string them through wooden beads. Tie a knot at the bottom of the beads.

6. Tie the bottoms of the string pieces to a second stick. Tie the tops of the string together to create a loop for hanging. Hang your funky feeder in a nearby tree!

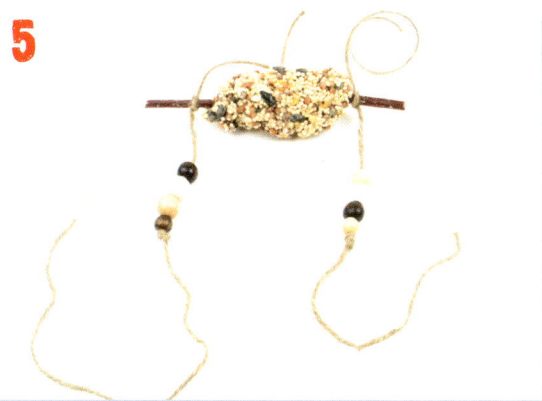

Keep crafting!

Form bird seed into fun shapes using cookie cutters! Poke tiny holes in the shapes to hang them up.

Flutter-by window sticker

Bird strikes, or birds flying into windows, cause millions of bird deaths every year. Help prevent bird strikes at your home and school with colourful window stickers!

Supplies

- pencil or felt-tip pen
- paper
- freezer bag
- black paint
- partly used bottle of white PVA glue
- wooden craft sticks or skewers
- cotton bud
- clear glue
- washing-up liquid
- measuring spoons
- food colouring
- small cups or dishes
- glitter
- paintbrushes

1. Use a pencil or felt-tip pen to draw flower designs on paper. Place the paper inside the freezer bag.

2. Add black paint to the glue bottle so that it is about one-third paint and two-thirds glue. Mix with a craft stick or skewer. Add more paint if needed to darken the colour.

3. Trace the designs onto the bag with the black glue mixture. Use a cotton swab to fix any mistakes. Let the designs dry overnight.

4. Use the craft stick to mix 30 ml clear glue, ¼ teaspoon washing-up liquid, and a drop or two of food colouring in a small cup or bowl. Repeat for any additional colours. Add glitter to each colour and stir.

5. Use paintbrushes to apply thick layers of the glue mixtures inside the black outlines on the bag. Let the designs dry overnight.

6. Carefully peel the clinging window stickers off the bag. Stick them to windows to warn birds to fly around the house or building!

CRAFTIVISM TIP

Make window stickers that spell out a kind message or a slogan for a cause that's important to you. Prevent bird crashes AND share your message with passers-by!

Seedlings to share

Plants offer countless benefits to the environment, such as increasing oxygen in the air, preventing soil erosion and providing food to humans and wildlife. Share the plant love with seedlings that others can plant in their homes!

Supplies

- egg box
- scissors
- soil or compost
- scoop or spoon
- seeds
- spray bottle of water
- wide craft sticks
- paint in two colours
- paintbrushes
- paint pen

1. Cut the lid off the egg box. Scoop soil into each section.

2. Use your finger to poke a hole in each section and drop in a seed. Cover the seeds with soil and spray the soil with water.

3. Keep the seedlings in sunlight. Every day, spray them with water until the soil is damp. Check the seed package for further care instructions.

4. When the seedlings have grown a few centimetres, cut the sections of the egg box apart.

5. Paint the top half of each craft stick in a solid colour. Leave them to dry. Add stripes, dots and other patterns with a different paint colour.

6. When the paint has dried, use a paint pen to write the seed type on the painted half of the craft sticks.

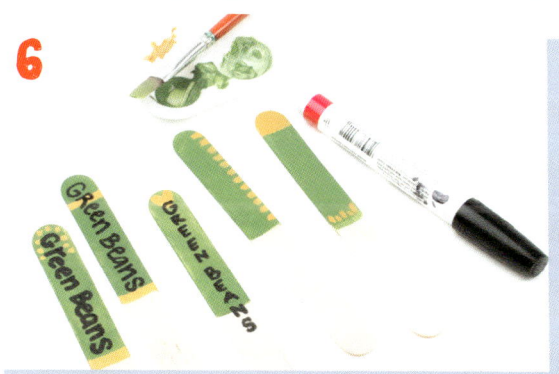

7. Add a labelled craft stick to each seedling. Give the seedlings to friends and family to plant in their gardens!

Keep crafting!

Green bean, radish, pumpkin, and marigold seeds are great for this project because they grow quickly. You can also look up ideas for what to plant based on your area and the time of year!

Seed bombs

Supplies
- 6 sheets construction paper
- 500 ml water
- blender
- strainer
- mixing bowl
- wildflower seeds
- plastic egg box or ice cube tray
- kitchen roll
- coloured card
- scissors
- felt-tip pen
- decorative paper
- PVA glue

Pollinators such as butterflies and bees are essential to the environment and human life. Help feed pollinators by planting colourful bursts of wildflowers!

1. Tear the coloured paper into small pieces and add them to the blender with the water. Blend the paper and water to form a smooth pulp.

2. Strain the pulp over the mixing bowl. Press out the extra water and pour it away.

3. Mix the pulp and seeds by hand in the mixing bowl. Press handfuls of pulp into each section of the egg box or ice cube tray.

4. Press down on the pulp sections with kitchen roll to dab away additional water. Allow the seed bombs to dry for 24 to 48 hours.

5. Cut rectangles out of coloured card. On one side, write the wildflower species you included in the seed bombs. Then write "Throw this seed bomb at a bare, sunny section of your lawn or garden. Water it and watch flowers burst to life!"

6. Cut flower shapes out of decorative paper. They should be large enough for a seed bomb to fit in the centre Use felt-tip pen to draw stems and leaves on the blank sides of the coloured card rectangles.

7. Glue the flower shapes to the rectangles above the stems. Glue the seed bombs to the flowers' centres. Give your seed bombs to friends, family and neighbours!

CRAFTIVISM TIP

You can also help pollinators by placing a water bowl filled with stones outside. The stones give pollinators a safe place to stand while they drink!

Cool composting

Solid waste in landfills emits harmful greenhouse gases. Composting can turn some solid waste into soil nutrients! Make a worktop composting bin. A filtered top limits odour. Drawings on the side remind you which items to compost!

Supplies

- coloured pencils
- construction paper
- black felt-tip pen
- scissors
- tissue paper
- 200 ml PVA glue
- 120 ml water
- measuring cups
- mixing bowl
- craft stick
- plastic container with lid
- paintbrush
- clear packing tape (optional)
- hammer and nail
- coffee filter

1. Use coloured pencils and construction paper to draw items that can be composted. These include apple cores, orange peels, teabags, coffee filters and leaves.

2. Outline the drawings in black felt-tip pen and cut them out.

3. Cut out small rectangles of tissue paper.

4. Use the craft stick to mix the glue and water in the mixing bowl. Brush the tissue paper pieces onto the container with the glue mixture and the paintbrush. Let the glue dry.

5. Stick the drawings onto the container. Brush the container with another layer of the glue mixture. Let the glue dry. If you'd like, cover the container in clear packing tape for an extra layer of protection.

6. Use the hammer and nail to poke holes in the lid.

7. Place the coffee filter inside the lid and screw on the top. Place compostable items in the container beneath the coffee filter. Then discard your compost in your garden or a local compost bin!

CRAFTIVISM TIP

Most towns and cities do food and garden waste collection services. You can also compost at home with a compost bin and other simple materials.

Earth cake pops

Hold a cake sale offering Earth-shaped cake pops! Donate the money you make selling these colourful creations to an environmental organization.

Ingredients

* 1 box cake mix
* ingredients and supplies listed on cake mix box
* 1 tub frosting
* white chocolate chips
* blue and green food colouring

Supplies

* mixing bowls
* rubber spatula
* cake tin
* baking tray or dish
* greaseproof paper
* tin foil
* microwave-safe bowls
* lollipop sticks
* spoon
* egg box
* toothpicks
* foam block, such as floral foam or recycled Styrofoam
* wrapping paper

1. Prepare and bake the cake according to the instructions on the cake mix package. Let the cake cool.

2. Use the rubber spatula to scoop the cake into a mixing bowl and crush it into crumbs. Add three-quarters of the frosting and mix until the frosting and crumbs are well combined.

3. With clean hands, shape the crumbs into balls about 4 cm in diameter. Place the cake balls on the greaseproof paper-lined baking tray or dish. Cover the pan with tin foil and refrigerate overnight.

Project continues on the next page.

4. Pour three-quarters of the white chocolate chips in the microwave-safe bowl. Microwave them in 30-second intervals, stirring in between each one, until the chocolate is melted and smooth.

5. Dip 1.5 cm of each lollipop stick into the melted chocolate and insert it into a cake ball.

6. Mix several drops of blue food colouring into the melted chocolate to create blue icing.

7. Dip each cake pop into the blue icing slowly, turning until it is completely covered. If needed, hold the cake pop over the bowl and spoon the icing onto it. Let excess icing drip back into the bowl.

8. Poke the cake pop sticks through the bottom of an egg box so the cake pops stand upright. Put the cake pops into the freezer until the icing sets.

9. Transfer the cake pops to a second greaseproof paper-lined baking tray or dish. Prepare the green icing. Melt the remaining chocolate chips in a microwave-safe bowl in 30-second intervals. Stir between each interval until the chocolate is melted and smooth. Stir in several drops of green food colouring.

10. Use a toothpick to apply the green icing to the cake pops in the shapes of continents. Once one side is complete, let the icing set in the freezer. Then rotate the cake pops and add green continents to the other side.

11. Wrap the block of foam in wrapping paper. Stick the cake pops in the foam to display them for a bake sale benefitting the environment!

CRAFTIVISM TIP

Write eco-friendly tips such as "Reduce, reuse, recycle" or "Plant a tree" on small strips of paper. Tape them around the lollipop sticks of each cake pop!

Vertical garden

Take advantage of every centimetre of outdoor space, including walls and fences! Like plants on the ground, plants in vertical gardens help filter pollutants from the air and absorb heat that would go into buildings.

Supplies

- 2 plastic fizzy drink or water bottles
- 2 tin cans or plastic pots
- craft knife
- hammer and nail
- corks (optional)
- paint and paintbrushes
- paint pens
- yarn
- yarn needle
- cactus potting soil
- succulents

1. Remove the labels from all the recycled containers.

2. With a craft knife, carefully cut large rectangles into the bottles. They should be large enough to fit at least one succulent but not so large that soil will spill out.

3. Opposite the rectangles in the bottles, cut two small Xs that line up with both short sides of the rectangle.

4. Use a hammer and nail to poke five hanging and drainage holes in the bottoms of the tins and pots. Make sure one hole is in the centre.

Project continues on the next page.

5. Place a cork in any plastic bottles missing their caps. Paint the containers in solid colours and leave to dry. Use paint pens to add patterns to the containers.

6. Cut two 1.8-m pieces of yarn. Tie a large knot in the end of each.

7. Use the yarn needle to thread one piece of yarn up through the centre hole in the bottom of a tin or pot. Tie a knot in the yarn several centimetres above where it comes out of the tin. Then thread the yarn through an X in one plastic bottle.

8. Tie a knot several centimetres above where the yarn comes out of the plastic bottle. Then thread the yarn through an X in the second plastic bottle.

9. Repeat steps 7 and 8 to thread the second piece of yarn through the other tin and the second Xs in both bottles.

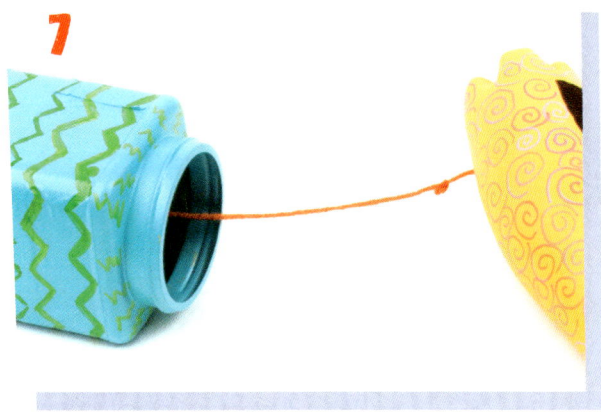

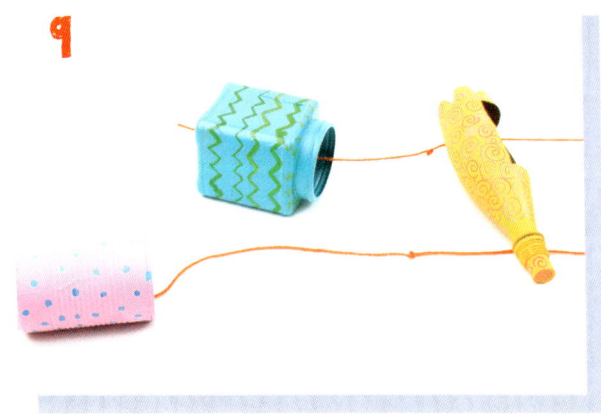

10. Cut the remaining yarn above the second bottle to the desired length and tie loops in the ends for hanging.

11. Fill each container with cactus potting soil. Plant succulents in each container, holding the yarn above it upright so the succulent doesn't push it down. Hang your vertical garden up outside so the succulents can soak up the Sun!

CRAFTIVISM TIP

Get permission from your local council to hang a vertical garden on a fence or wall at a nearby park.

Self-watering planter pals

These self-watering planters aren't just cute and silly! They also protect your plants by keeping them hydrated and preventing overwatering.

Supplies

- plastic bottles
- sandpaper
- craft knife or scissors
- paint and paintbrushes
- air-dry clay
- googly eyes
- hot glue gun
- duct tape
- hammer and nail
- string
- potting soil
- scoop
- small plants
- water

1. Rub the surfaces of the bottles with sandpaper to help paint stick to them.

2. Use the craft knife or scissors to cut off the top third of each bottle.

3. Paint the bottles in solid colours. Leave a vertical strip on the bottle bases unpainted so you can check water levels later on. Let the bottles dry. Then flip the tops of the bottles upside down and set them into the bases.

4. Use air-dry clay to sculpt eyelids, eyebrows, feet, lips, noses, beaks and other features. The planters can be animals, humans or monsters! Put the features aside and let the clay dry overnight.

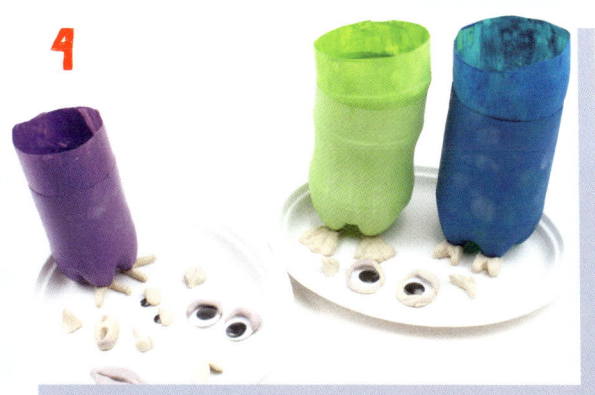

Project continues on the next page.

5. Paint the clay features and let them dry. Using the hot glue gun, glue the features to the planter bases opposite the vertical strip.

6. Paint more details onto the planter bases if you would like.

7. Use duct tape to create eyelashes or feathers. Glue them to the planter bases using the hot glue gun.

8. Use the hammer and nail to poke a hole in each of the bottle lids.

9. Cut a length of string about 30 cm long and tie a large knot in the end. Pull the string through the hole in the lid. The string will pull water from the base of the planter and water the plant on top. Screw the lid onto the bottle.

10. Scoop potting soil into the planter tops. Remove the plants from their containers and place them into the planters. Top the planters with additional soil.

11. Water the plants. Then fill the base with water. Place your plants in a sunny spot and check on their water levels regularly. Refill the bases when the string can no longer reach the water!

Keep crafting!

Craft extra-large, self-watering planters with 2.27-litre (4-pint) milk cartons or orange juice bottles.

Find out more

Books

Recycle and Remake: Creative Projects for Eco Kids (DK Children, 2020)

Recycle It! (Saving Our Planet), Mary Boone (Raintree, 2020)

Upcycled Plastic Projects (Eco Crafts), Marcy Morin and Heidi E. Thompson (Raintree, 2022)

Websites

www.bbc.co.uk/cbbc/curations/bp-arts-and-crafts-collection
Love crafting? Head for the CBBC Blue Peter arts and crafts collection.

www.goodhousekeeping.com/holidays/g39314721/earth-day-crafts-for-kids/
This website has 40 fun crafting projects to help you celebrate Earth Day.

www.natgeokids.com/uk/discover/science/nature/how-to-save-the-planet/
National Geographic Kids gives you ideas to help save the planet.

About the author

Ruthie Van Oosbree is a writer and editor who loves making crafts. She is passionate about social justice, animal welfare and the environment. She lives with her husband and three adorable cats in Minnesota, USA.